MEN-AT-ARMS SERIE[S]

EDITOR: PHILIP WARNE[R]

Wellington's Peninsular Army

Text by JAMES LAWFORD

Colour plates by MICHAEL ROFFE

Research for uniforms and illustrations T. A. HEATHCOTE

HIPPOCRENE
BOOKS, INC.

Hippocrene Books, Inc.
171 Madison Avenue
New York, N.Y. 10016

First published in the United States 1973
ISBN 0-88254-170-6

First published in Great Britain in 197 by
Osprey Publishing Ltd, P.O. Box 25,
707 Oxford Road, Reading, Berkshire

Printed in Great Britain

The Staff

During Marlborough's Wars at the beginning of the eighteenth century the muskets of the infantry and the guns of the artillery were smooth-bore and muzzle-loading, cavalry relied on shock tactics and the sabre, engineers based their fortifications on the principles of Vauban. When Wellington took the field nearly a hundred years later weapons had barely altered; a few British infantry were armed with the new-fangled rifle which the French had not thought worth adopting, and a few French or Polish/French cavalry regiments used the lance as well as the sabre, guns fired projectiles that were a little heavier than before and were slightly more mobile, while the technique of fortifications and sieges remained completely unchanged. Over the century weapon technology had hardly advanced at all. But paradoxically, perhaps in part from the very fact that weapons had altered so little permitting their characteristics to be thoroughly understood, perhaps in part because large regular armies remained continuously in existence, during that century military theory, organizationally, tactically and strategically, made remarkable progress. After the forcing-house of the Napoleonic wars, European armies reached levels of technical excellence which have probably never been surpassed, perhaps never equalled. The theories of Clausewitz, which were to dominate military thought for the next century and more, were almost entirely based on the detailed analysis he and other military thinkers made of the principles underlying the great battles of the Napoleonic period.

At the beginning of this period the record of the British army left something to be desired. But during the Peninsular War, 1808–14, Wellington led and trained a British army that, fighting against the French, the masters of Europe, never knew a major defeat in the field. Wellington himself, whose terse unflattering comments on his men have long been remembered, described his army as 'able to go anywhere or do anything.'

The staff by which he controlled his magnificent army reflected his own personality and the conditions of the time. Battlefields were small and regiments fought close together; generals could assemble all their men in a single place and transmit their orders by the power of their lungs; there was no need for the elaborate staff organizations of a later day. Napoleon it is true, co-ordinating the activities of a number of armies operating

Arthur Wellesley, Duke of Wellington. He was thirty-eight years old when, in 1808, as Sir Arthur Wellesley, he first landed in the Peninsula and forced the French out of Portugal.

The Battle of Fuentes de Onoro, British Headquarters. A staff officer is galloping off with a message. Wellington, wearing his usual low cocked hat and plain frock-coat, is attended by a light dragoon and other staff officers. In the background Royal Horse Artillery are changing ground (After St Clair)

hundreds of miles apart, evolved the idea of a chief-of-staff who could interpret and elaborate directions from the commander and even possibly assist him in his planning. Wellington desired nothing of this; he wanted advice or assistance from no one; modern planning staffs would have filled him with horror. In his view the formulating of plans and giving out of orders were the responsibility of the commanders. Staff officers were there to transmit these orders and to smooth out minor administrative difficulties.

In consequence, in Wellington's headquarters there was no eqivalent of the general staff. He had a small personal staff under a lieutenant-colonel to handle his military correspondence, but the colonel was a secretary, nothing more. The most important branch of the staff was the department of the Quarter-Master-General. It was headed by a major-general and initially consisted of a small group of officers, perhaps twelve in number (as the army grew bigger so their numbers increased) in addition an officer from the department served in each division.

The duties of these officers extended to such matters as quartering, the moving of equipment the layout of camps, duties differing little from those of the present day; but their duties also included some of those now discharged by the general staff such as mapping, the compiling of information about the countryside and its resources, the organizing of all forms of movement and the drafting of orders. The Quarter-Master General's department provided the executive staff of the army, so far as such may be said to have existed.

The other great department was that of the Adjutant-General, also under a major-general Initially this comprised fourteen officers but with the passage of time this number too increased again a staff officer from the department served

4

with each division. The responsibilities of these officers included such matters as discipline, statistics about unit strengths, reinforcements etc., and differed little from those of the modern 'A' staff.

The distinctions between the two departments were by no means rigid and an officer from one might well find himself deputizing for an absentee from the other. But one thing Wellington made absolutely clear, the function of the staff officer was to transmit the instructions of his commander, he had no right to arrogate to himself the authority of his general.

Besides the staff proper, Wellington kept in his headquarters the field commanders of his engineers, artillery and medical services. In addition Marshal Beresford, the Commander-in-Chief of the Portuguese army, after one disastrous experience commanding an army at Albuera, generally accompanied army headquarters, as did Sir Stapleton Cotton, from 1812 onwards the commander of the cavalry in the Peninsula. Thus Wellington had with him two senior generals whom he could send off at a moment's notice to take over an independent command or disentangle some unfortunate situation; it gave him a flexibility that allowed him to dispense with the system of Army Corps originated by the French.

On the civil side there was an important department, the Commissariat, under a Commissary General with assistants serving with every division and brigade. These were responsible for the provision of rations and the procurement of all local produce. In the nature of things a thin or ill-provided commissary officer was rarely seen, and they were apt to receive more kicks than credit.

Working direct to Army Headquarters were the divisions; there was only an intermediate headquarters when two or more were grouped together for an independent task. Here staffs were kept to the minimum. Leith Hay, an A.D.C. with the 5th Division, records that at the Battle of Salamanca the divisional staff consisted of Colonel Berkeley, probably Assistant-Quarter-Master-General, and Major Gomm, probably Deputy-Assistant-Adjutant-General, and four A.D.C.s, possibly one per brigade and one to look after the domestic arrangements of the headquarters.

Marshal Beresford in hand-to-hand combat with a Polish lancer at Albuera. He was a man of immense physical strength and the lancer had short shrift

The high sounding titles for staff officers have been retained to the present day, generally abbreviated to the initials, thereby ensuring that the army staff should be confusing to the other services and incomprehensible to other nations.

At the level of the infantry brigade, there was a single staff officer, the major of brigade; he was a captain or sometimes an able young subaltern drawn from one of its regiments. During the later stages of the war, when regimental officers had recognized the wisdom of wearing the same type of headdress as their men, staff officers could be distinguished by their courageous refusal to abandon the traditional cocked hat.

The Infantry

When Wellington took the field in the Peninsula in 1808, Britain lagged behind France in the higher organization of her armies, divisions had yet to be formed, and Wellington dealt direct with individual brigade commanders. In June 1809, however, he adopted the divisional organization originated by the French, in which a number of brigades were grouped together under a single commander. Initially he formed four divisions, but by 1812 the number had risen to eight British and one Portuguese; he numbered his British divisions consecutively from one to seven, the eighth, the most famous, was known simply as the Light Division. Each was commanded by a lieutenant-general and usually comprised three brigades; two of which were British, each under a major-general, and one foreign, often under a British brigadier-general – a rank otherwise seldom encountered in the Peninsular Army.

There were some exceptions. All three brigades of the 2nd Division were British, but since it normally operated with General Hamilton's Portuguese Division, both under the command of Wellington's most trusted subordinate, General 'Daddy' Hill, the two together virtually amounted to the equivalent of a small Anglo-Portuguese Army Corps. In the 1st Division the foreign brigade was from the King's German Legion recruited by George III from the remnants of his Hanoverian Army, in the remainder (except for the Light Division which had a peculiar organization of its own) it came from the Portuguese Army

General Lord Hill, wearing the uniform of the post Napoleonic period

which had been reorganized under the command of Marshal Beresford and stiffened by British officers who had transferred to the Portuguese service.

The composition of the Light Division derived from an essential feature of Wellington's tactics. He had served under the Duke of York in Flanders where he had noted how the French light troops, their Tirailleurs and Voltigeurs, could harass and weaken a battle line, so that when the heavy French columns attacked it they often broke through. He resolved to counter this gambit by deploying forward of his positions such a mass of his own light troops that the Tirailleurs and Voltigeurs would be held well short of his main position. As a first step towards achieving this aim, he constituted the Light Division with the function of screening the army both at rest and on the move. It consisted of only two small brigades each containing a Caçadore battalion (Portuguese Light Infantry) four companies of riflemen from the 95th (later increased when the 2nd and 3rd battalions of that regiment joined his army) and a British light infantry battalion (the role in which the 43rd and 52nd won immortal fame).

The 7th Division also was rather unusual; perhaps at first Wellington toyed with the idea of producing another light infantry division: it had two light infantry brigades, one containing two light battalions of the King's German Legion and nine rifle companies of the Brunswick Oel Jägers and the other two newly trained British light infantry battalions, the 51st and the 68th, and a battalion originally recruited from French emigrés and deserters, the Chasseurs Britannique, a regiment famous for the speed with which its men deserted; in addition there was the normal Portuguese brigade. This division, perhaps owing to its diversity of races, never won much renown; the malicious affected to disbelieve in its very existence, and in 1813 it reverted to a more normal organization, the light infantry battalions from the King's German Legion being transferred to the 1st Division.

In the British brigades there were generally three line battalions. Occasionally a fourth might be added, and in Guards Brigades, since a battalion of Foot Guards invariably outnumbered by a considerable margin those of the line, there were only two. On average a brigade numbered about 2,000 men, but sickness and casualties, or the arrival of a strong battalion, could cause wide fluctuations. The Portuguese brigades followed the continental model and embodied a Caçadore battalion and two line regiments each of two battalions; these had seven companies and an authorized strength of 750, but rarely put more than 500 in the field; even so, Portuguese brigades on average numbered 2,500 and were almost always larger than the British.

The organization of the British battalions remained remarkably constant throughout the war. Each was commanded by a lieutenant-colonel and consisted of a grenadier company, a light company, and eight line companies, all commanded by captains. The colonel had two majors serving under him, nominally to command the two wings into which the battalion was customarily split; their main function, however, was to deputize for him when he was away and to take charge of any large detachments the battalion might be called upon to make; within the battalion their duties tended to depend on the particular whims or eccentricities of their commanders.

In the companies, the captains had under them two junior officers, in theory a lieutenant and an ensign, but there was no set proportion between the two ranks. A full-strength battalion, therefore, would be commanded by a lieutenant-colonel with under him two majors, ten captains, twenty lieutenants or ensigns, the adjutant, (generally a lieutenant), and the quarter-master; an assistant surgeon was normally attached. Sir David Dundas shows the strength of a company as being three officers, two sergeants, three corporals, one drummer, and thirty privates. This must have been at the peace-time establishment of one platoon. At war establishment, another platoon

Portuguese infantry at Penmacor 18 March 1811. (St Clair) The mounted officers wearing the 'stove-pipe' shako are below field rank. The pioneers are wearing bearskin caps and leather aprons. Their axes are not visible. The drummers carry their drums slung on their backs by means of the drum cords. (The length of the drum cord was governed by this requirement)

7

was added without any increase in the number of officers. When going to the Peninsula companies might number nearly 100 including a pay sergeant, perhaps four other sergeants and six corporals. The 52nd went to the Peninsula with 54 sergeants and about 850 rank and file. But sickness and other casualties soon took their toll, and when in 1810 the 2nd battalion of the 52nd disbanded its total strength was 20 sergeants, 12 buglers, and 572 rank and file of whom 10 sergeants, 5 buglers, and 85 rank and file were unfit for duty.

A battalion with 700 men present in the field was looked on as strong, many fell well below this figure, and some had little more than 500. In a battalion of 700 men, deducting the musicians, the adjutant's batman, the clerks, the storemen and others of that ilk likely to find their way into headquarters – say forty men – there would be 660 men serving with the companies; allowing again for the various duties that inexorably sap the strength of a regiment such as baggage guards, storemen, men just gone sick, absentees and so on, the company could probably put not much more than fifty-five men into the line. Captain Sherer remarked that at the Battle of Vitoria he had eleven casualties out of a company of thirty-eight and does not comment that at this time his company strength was abnormally low. The company for administrative purposes was divided into two platoons, but organizations were far from standardized and commanding officers were often men of character who liked to run their battalions after their own fashion and did not welcome interference from the nincompoops of the staff. The private soldier in the ranks carried sixty rounds of ball ammunition, a knapsack, a haversack, rolled blanket or great coat, a full waterbottle and probably some other articles he had managed to acquire; his load might amount to nearly sixty pounds. At first the heavy camp-kettles for cooking were carried on a company mule, but when, in 1812, Wellington managed to issue tents to his men at a scale of three twelve-men bell-tents per company, the tents were carried on the mule and a lighter type of camp-kettle was carried in turn by the men of the company.

Their clothing and in particular that of the officers might be curious and fanciful and be only remotely related to the regulation pattern; Wellington himself never worried over such matters so long as his men resembled soldiers and would not be mistaken for the French.

'BROWN BESS'

Officers were armed with the sword, and sergeants with halberds or short pikes, called spontoons, rather to assist them in dressing the ranks than as weapons of offence. Most of the soldiers were armed with the musket, affectionately known as Brown Bess, that the Duke of Marlborough when Master-General of the Ordnance was said to have introduced. Its barrel was about 42 inches long with a diameter of ·75 of an inch; its firing mechanism was reputedly the most reliable in Europe, although at this time that was not necessarily a very great feat; its heavy triangular bayonet, 17 inches long, fitted on the barrel well clear of the muzzle. Each soldier carried his 60 rounds of ball made up into cartridges, the propelling charge and the ball being sewn together in cartridge paper to make a small cylindrical parcel. When the time came to load, the soldier bit the end of the cartridge, shook a little powder on his priming pan and emptied the rest down the barrel; he then used his ramrod to ram home his ball with the cartridge paper on top to act as a wadding. When he pulled the trigger a spark from the flint ignited the powder in the pan which in turn caused the powder in the barrel to explode; the proportion of misfires, however, could be as high as one in six and, if the powder became damp, the musket would not fire at all.

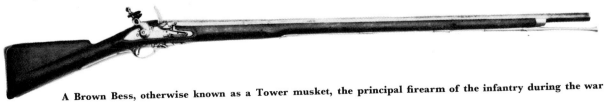

A Brown Bess, otherwise known as a Tower musket, the principal firearm of the infantry during the war

Manual Exercise according to the late regulation by the Duke of York.
See Treatise on Military Affairs.

1 Prime & Load   2 Handle Cartridge   3 Prime

4 Load   5 Draw Ramrod   6 Ram down Cartridge

Loading and firing, from a manual of musketry exercises. The uniform is that of an earlier period; the hat had been replaced by the 'stove-pipe' shako in 1796, and the coat by the single-breasted short-tailed coatee. White gaiters continued to be worn only by the Foot Guards in full dress

The ball was not always a very close fit in the barrel, and the gases from the exploding charge might escape around it making it spin and swerve wildly in flight. Brown Bess had a certain feminine capriciousness; at fifty yards it could be aimed with some hope of success; up to two hundred yards it could be usefully fired at a group, the man actually aimed at being almost certain to escape harm; but over 200 yards, although the ball could carry up to 700, its behaviour was so eccentric that the noise of the discharge was more likely to excite terror than the ball. Rates of fire depended on how thoroughly the soldier performed his loading drills and the care that he took when he aimed; he could fire up to five rounds a minute if he was satisfied with producing an imposing number of bangs without worrying overmuch what happened to his ball; taking into account battle conditions a well-trained soldier should have been capable of firing nearly three effective rounds a minute.

Owing to the relative inaccuracy of the musket, the high number of misfires, and also the moral effect of a sudden blast of fire, a volley from a number of men was likely to produce a more awe-inspiring result than a comparable number of single shots, and the more concentrated the fire the more devastating it was likely to be; hence, throughout most of the eighteenth century, soldiers stood shoulder to shoulder in a line that was three ranks deep; the French experimented with four but found that the fire of the fourth was more likely to endanger their comrades than the enemy. At this time the three-deep line was still the normal practice on the continent as it gave the line a certain solidity and catered for the replacement of casualties.

TACTICS

During the War of American Independence, especially in wild country against irregular bodies

9

Pombal, 11 March 1811 (St Clair). Infantry on the approach march. Company officers wearing shakos have dismounted. The Colours, uncased, are in the middle of the column. An officer of the light company (wings on his shoulders) is talking to one of the staff.

of riflemen, the British army had become accustomed to a looser order. Battalions frequently fought in only two ranks and these were not properly closed up by European standards; this was beneficial in that it led Wellington to adopt a two-rank line in the Peninsula, but with the loose order regiments had come to devise tactical manoeuvres of their own and drill had become sloppy and haphazard; the results in Flanders had not always been happy. In 1792 the Duke of York, the Commander-in-Chief, decided that a common tactical doctrine must be adopted by the whole of the infantry and issued a manual entitled *Rules and Regulations for the Field Formation Exercise of Movements of His Majesty's Forces*, which he proceeded rigorously to enforce. The manual, written by Sir David Dundas, was largely based on formations current in the Prussian army and has been reviled as intolerably rigid in outlook; nevertheless it gave a sound tactical doctrine to the infantry and was the basis of the battle-drills used in the Peninsula.

Dundas envisaged the men in a battalion standing shoulder to shoulder in a line three ranks deep. (As already mentioned, Wellington reduced this to two.) The first part of his manual was devoted to the individual drills such as turning, marching and wheeling, that the soldier had to master before he was fit to take his place in his company. In the remainder he laid down a series of drills which, while retaining the rigid, slow-moving line as the battle formation yet enabled a battalion to move swiftly and easily over the battlefield. He divided the battalion into eight equal divisions; these roughly corresponded to the eight line companies if the grenadier and light companies were both excluded; if they were present he allowed the number of divisions to be increased to ten; on the other hand if the battalion was weak the number could be reduced proportionately. In practice it was rare for the light company to form part of the battle line; its

A brigade fording the Mondego, 1810 (St Clair). An example of a brigade advancing with its battalions in column of divisions. The divisions seem well closed up, probably to hasten the crossing.

normal task was to screen the front or flanks of the battalion or brigade. The grenadier company, no longer specifically armed with grenades, was composed of the steadiest soldiers in the unit; it might be used for some particularly dangerous or difficult task, but the habit of brigading the grenadier companies to make up *ad hoc* grenadier battalions had largely disappeared. In some regiments the grenadier company was divided, half being placed on the right and half on the left of the line. Dundas does not seem to have thought that any specific provision was necessary for its deployment.

Although he described some eighteen man-oeuvres in detail, in essence his drills were based on four key formations, column of route, column of divisions, line and square. Column of route was used for all movement when there was no im-mediate threat of contact with the enemy. Dundas laid down that this could be carried out in fours if the line formed two deep, sixes if three deep. Since marching men required double the space occupied by the men when stationary, the length of a column of route should equal the frontage of the same unit in line, and he em-phasized that this length should not be exceeded. March discipline much resembled that in force in the British Army until the 1930s when the threat from the air enforced a greater degree of dispersion. Battalions started off from their camping grounds with arms at the slope or shoulder and bands playing. After a short distance the men marched at ease and were per-mitted to break step. At every clock hour there was a short halt to enable the men to rest and adjust their equipment. Before the hourly halt and immediately after it, men marched to atten-tion and in step for a few minutes, and the same drill was observed when they arrived at their destination or were called upon to execute a manoeuvre.

When contact with the enemy became a possi-

11

bility, column of route was changed to column of divisions, or if the company organization had been preserved, column of companies. In this formation each division deployed in a two-deep line with the divisions ranged one behind the other, No. 1 Division leading; occasionally it might be convenient to have No. 8 in front. Here two rather confusing terms were apt to be used. If No. 1 led, the battalion was said to be 'right in front' if No. 8 'left in front', the terms referring to their respective positions when in line. In some circumstances it was desirable to adopt a compromise between column and line. For this purpose Dundas had enacted that besides being divided into eight divisions, the battalion line should also be divided into four grand divisions, and column of grand divisions, generally formed by grouping in pairs, might be substituted for column of divisions.

Intervals might be varied. In close column there might be only seven paces between the front rank of one division and the front rank of the one immediately behind it. On the move open column was more usual; in this formation the distance between divisions was equal to their front for an important reason; with these intervals the battalion could form line facing left or right very quickly indeed, as each division needed to do no more than execute a separate right or left wheel for the whole to be in line. This was the manoeuvre so brilliantly executed by Pakenham and the 3rd Division at the battle of Salamanca. Forming line to the front was a slower process. Each division came up in succession on the right or left of the division in front of it, depending on the flank ordered, until the line had been formed, while the leading division normally halted to

The Battle of Castalla. A British infantry battalion in line faces an attack by French infantry in column. On the hill the colonel rides in his correct position behind the Colours. One of the majors has been wounded and fallen off his horse; the other (cocked hat and dismounted) brings up a company on the right. Company officers (shakos, straight swords) are in their positions on the flanks of their companies. In the right foreground a light infantry officer brings up his reserve in close order to support his skirmishers. The light infantry bugler, one trusts, is sounding the advance while a French drummer is probably responding with the 'pas de charge'. (Light infantry, often working dispersed, used bugles not drums for the passage of orders)

allow the others to catch up; the rear division might therefore find it had some 200 yards to cover, and if, as sometimes happened, the whole brigade was advancing in column of companies or divisions this distance might be tripled.

Once in line, the colours took post in the centre with the Colonel, mounted, six paces behind. The senior major and the adjutant, also mounted, took post respectively behind the 3rd and 6th Divisions; the company commanders, dismounted, took up a position on the right of the front rank of their company or division with a sergeant covering them in the rear rank. The remaining officers and sergeants, the drummers, pioneers and any other hangers-on formed a third supernumerary rank with orders as Dundas phrased it to 'keep the others closed up to the front during the attack and prevent any break beginning in the rear'. The second-in-command of the left-hand division, however, covered by a sergeant, took post on the left flank of that division.

When advancing in line the men on the flanks kept their alignment by dressing on the colours in the centre. If a brigade advanced in line it was the duty of the colour parties to align themselves on the colours of the particular battalion that had been detailed to set pace and direction. In this formation the senior battalion was on the right the next senior on the left and the junior in the centre.

The last formation, that of square, Dundas shows as being formed from line. With No. 1 Division on the right and No. 8 on the left the procedure was as follows. The 4th and 5th Divisions stood fast, the 2nd and 3rd wheeled to their right rear forming a line at right angles to the right flank of No. 4 Division, while the 6th and 7th in a similar manner wheeled to their left rear forming a line at right angles to the left flank of No. 5 Division. The 1st and 8th Divisions closed the square and faced the rear; the officers and colours took post in its centre, the officers waving their swords exultantly in the air whenever a volley was fired.

There were many other drills for forming square; sometimes it was formed in two ranks, sometimes in four; on occasion two battalions might unite, as at Waterloo, to make up a single square. When two or more squares were necessary,

A British infantry square being attacked by lancers

alternate ones would be echelonned back, so that the fire from one could sweep the face of the next. It is evident that if a square were to be formed quickly and without confusion, companies had to be of equal strength, and that some system, such as that of divisions, was probably unavoidable. Nevertheless, the advantages of the fighting unit and the administrative being identical, so that officers and N.C.O.s knew the men they led in action, became more and more apparent, and the custom of using the company as the tactical unit became steadily more widespread as the war progressed.

To give still greater flexibility in manoeuvre, Dundas decreed that a division should be divided into two sub-divisions and four sections, but added that a section should never number less than five files (fifteen men if the ranks were three deep); these would operate the same formations within a division as a division within a battalion. As the division was the smallest sub-unit under an officer it may be surmised that these smaller formations were rarely used, unless a company was operating independently on its own.

As regards frontages, Dundas stated that a man should occupy twenty-two inches. Two feet, however, would seem a more realistic figure, besides being easier to use for purposes of calculation. A battalion 700 strong, subtracting the light company, the musicians, and those in the supernumerary third rank, would probably muster about 560 men actually in the battle line; assuming a front rank of 280, the frontage for such a battalion would be in the region of 200 yards. Since a brigade normally fought with all three battalions in line its front would extend about

The Regimental Colour. The colour parties of the infantry carried two flags each borne by an ensign or subaltern and known as the First or Royal Colour and the Regimental Colour. The First Colour was a Union Jack with the regimental number in its centre; the Regimental was more complicated. Its background colour matched the facings of the regiment; in its right-hand corner there was a small Union Jack and in its centre a red shield containing the regimental number or emblem, normally surrounded by a wreath of the union flowers, the rose, thistle and shamrock. Other honours might be painted on it. In the illustration the officer has removed the staff from its socket and is carrying the colour partially furled; its oilskin case can be seen over his right shoulder. A sergeant in the party stands close to defend the nearly helpless officer with his spontoon

600 yards. Infantry divisions on the other hand seldom had all three brigades in line. At the Battle of Salamanca the 4th Division did so with disastrous results; Wellington had, however, with customary prescience placed the 6th Division behind it to give the attack depth, and Cole commanding the 4th may well have taken this into account when determining his formation.

When the manoeuvring had ended and the fighting had begun it was important that at no time should a battalion be discovered with all its muskets unloaded; if this should happen it would be helpless before cavalry, and enemy infantry would be able to close and blast it off the battlefield with impunity. Dundas frowned on file firing whereby each front rank and rear rank man fired immediately after the man on his right, and favoured the firing of volleys. He stated: 'Line will fire by platoons, each battalion independent, and firing beginning from the centre of each.' In his regulations Dundas uses the terms platoon and company as though they were the same, and presumably meant here that firing would be by company or division; since there was only one officer in the front rank of each division, except for the left flank one, it seems logical to suppose that these were the units of fire; on the other hand it is likely that battalions developed procedures of their own. After the first volley men almost certainly fired independently as fast as possible, the initial method of opening fire ensuring that firing remained continuous. At close range this fire could be murderous; after two or three minutes one side would almost certainly begin to fall into disorder, and seeing this the other would probably clinch matters with the bayonet. Captain Sherer describing his action at the Battle of Albuera gives some idea of what the reality must have been like:

Just as our line had entirely cleared the Spaniards, the smoky shroud of battle was, by the slackening of fire, for one minute blown aside, and gave to our view the French grenadier caps, their arms, and the whole aspect of their frowning masses. It was a momentary, but a grand sight; a heavy atmosphere of smoke again enveloped us, and few objects could be discerned at all, none distinctly. The murderous contest of musketry lasted long. We were the whole time advancing on and shaking the enemy. At the distance of about twenty yards from them we received orders to charge. We ceased firing, cheered and had our bayonets in the charging position . . . The French infantry broke and fled, abandoning some guns and howitzers about sixty yards from us . . . To describe my feelings throughout this wild scene with fidelity would be impossible: at intervals a shriek or a groan told that men were falling about me; but it was not always that the tumult of the contest suffered me to catch these sounds. A constant feeling [i.e. closing] to the centre of our line and the gradual diminution of our front more truly bespoke the havoc of death.

For a battalion the sequence of action might be an approach march in column of route, then a

The 57th Foot (West Middlesex Regiment), 'the die-hards', at the Battle of Albuera. Grenadier caps were commonly worn by the drummers and the colours of their coatees were the reverse of those of their regiments; in this case the coatee was yellow with red facings

halt at an assembly area where the battalion might close up in column of grand divisions, and stand poised ready to swing into action. Here colours would be uncased and primings checked. Then would come the advance in open column, deployment into line and finally trial by fire.

During the later stages of the advance the light infantry might well have been deployed in front; while capable of taking their place in the battle line, they generally had other more important functions to perform. They were equipped with a lighter version of the Brown Bess that had a barrel only thirty-nine inches long. They always acted in pairs – from the time he joined his unit each man had to choose a comrade from whom he was separated neither in camp nor on the battlefield. When a light infantry company operated on its own a few men would be kept in close order as a reserve immediately under the hand of the commander, the rest would be spread in pairs across the front, one member of each a little in front of his comrade so that they could cover each other either advancing or retiring; the intervals between pairs would vary from two to twelve paces depending on the extent of the front they had to cover. These skirmishers, as they were called, preserved only the roughest of lines, selecting individual firing positions where the best cover could be obtained. Being widely separated, they worked to bugle calls like the cavalry, not the drums of the line. In an advance they would close with the enemy's line and while themselves presenting an insignificant target, gall it unmercifully with their fire. In defence they had to present an impenetrable front to the light troops of the enemy; but, once attacked in force, their task was done and they were permitted to withdraw to a flank, taking the utmost care not to mask the fire of their own line as they went. Light companies might work independently, but more often those in a brigade were grouped together under a single commander to form a small light infantry unit, and in the Portuguese brigade all the light companies were already concentrated in the Caçadore battalion.

In front of the light infantry the riflemen, the élite of the skirmishers, might be seen weaving their way forward. Initially Wellington had three rifle battalions, the 95th, the 5th/60th Rifles and the Brunswick Oel Jägers. Later these were increased by the arrival of two more battalions of the 95th, and in addition a number of rifles were made available to the Light Battalions of the King's German Legion. (Oman has stated that the Caçadore battalions were armed with rifles and a number of authorities agree with him. However, taking into account the total production of the Baker rifle in the United Kingdom, the

Riflemen of the 95th covering the right flank of the line. The short brass-hilted sword they carried in lieu of a bayonet, and the powder horn under the right arm, show up clearly

contention is open to doubt. Possibly some Caçadore battalions were so armed.) All were armed with the Baker rifle, a muzzle-loader with a barrel 30 inches long and ·615 inches diameter; to load it the ball had to be forced home against the resistance of the rifling grooves, a serious handicap which limited the rate of fire to approximately one round a minute. However, the rifle was sufficiently accurate for aimed fire to be possible at ranges of up to 200 yards, four times the range of a musket, and effective fire at 300 yards was by no means uncommon.

Wellington always allotted at least one company of riflemen to each infantry division; they operated ahead of everyone, slinking from cover to cover like hunters or poachers, rather than the brightly-hued soldiers of the day, and they were the first troops to wear an elementary form of camouflage clothing. The 60th having been raised as the Royal American Regiment wore green to match the forests where they had origi-

nated and the 95th did the same; the Brunswick Oel Jägers wore black, but this was partially to mourn for the rape of Brunswick by Napoleon, while the Caçadores, when not clothed by the British in rifle green, wore brown, perhaps the earliest use of a version of khaki.

Wellington looked to his infantry for his victories and indeed initially with few guns and less cavalry he was given little choice. Perhaps in consequence, although in two of his greatest battles, those of Vitoria and Salamanca, he was the attacker, he won his greatest renown as the master of defence. When selecting his position for a defensive battle he selected a ridge, wherever possible, deploying his troops below its crest and out of sight of the enemy. French commanders encountering such a position rarely saw more than a few scattered guns with small groups of light infantry dotting the forward slopes, who discouraged close reconnaissance by accurate fire at remarkably long ranges. When the French came to launch their attack, their massed artillery, unable to see a true target, would be largely ineffective, while their skirmishers would fail to dislodge Wellington's light infantry; then, when their heavy columns, groping their way uncertainly up the ridge through a swarm of skirmishers, finally reached the crest they would suddenly find in front of them a long steady scarlet wall of infantry and their leading files would be blown away before they had recovered from their surprise. Even as late as the closing stages of the Battle of Waterloo, Napoleon's Imperial Guard thought they had broken through the British line only for the Foot Guards to emerge out of a cornfield, and drastically enlighten them. It is probable that infantry have never been handled with greater skill than under Wellington and equally that no general was better served by his infantry soldiers.

6th Inniskilling Dragoon officer, 1814, in review order. The epaulette on the right shoulder is hidden but the crimson waist sash, a distinction of commissioned rank, is clearly visible. On active service overalls replaced boots and breeches, and the ornate sabretache (the purse-like object hanging down behind his left leg) was replaced by one of black leather

The Cavalry

Paradoxically enough, the basic organization of a cavalry regiment bore a marked similarity to that of an infantry battalion. It was commanded by a lieutenant-colonel with two majors, ten captains and twenty lieutenants or cornets under him; it consisted of ten troops, each under a captain, and had a war establishment of about eighty privates (the term trooper was not then used) and eighty horses. From time to time there were minor variations in the numbers, but substantially these figures held good for the whole period of the war.

The number of men actually present with the regiment, especially after a long period in the field, was considerably less. In *Rules and Regulations for the Cavalry, 1796* for instance, it was directed that 'Each troop should be divided into two squads when under forty, into three or more when above, according to the number, with an equal number of non-commissioned officers in each . . . The squads must be as separate and distinct as

possible . . . The squad is entirely in charge of its own sergeant.' This seems to have relieved the junior officers of all administrative responsibilities. However, they were ordered to 'look in on the men at dinner hours', regrettably not so much to check the quality of the rations as to see that their men 'do not dispose of their meat for liquor'. In an optimistic vein the Regulations continued, 'nor is any dragoon to give way to that blackguard practice of swearing'. Officers too, had to preserve a certain decorum and the Regulations emphasized, 'on no account is an officer to wear his hat on the back of his head'.

In some minor ways the cavalry organization took into account the differences of that arm from the infantry. The senior non-commissioned-officer in a troop was the troop quartermaster and in regimental headquarters there was a riding master with rough riders under him to train horses and men. As in the infantry there was an adjutant and a sergeant-major; the latter's duties included

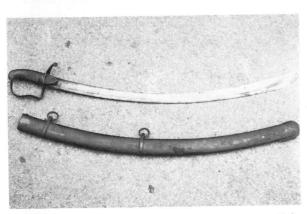

Light cavalry pattern trooper's sabre carried by light dragoons and hussars throughout the war; heavy dragoons carried a straight sword

drilling the young officers and these had to pay him a guinea and a half for the privilege of listening to his words of counsel couched, no doubt, in traditional terms.

Cavalry regiments fell into two main categories, heavy and light. The distinction at this time had little significance so far as their duties in the field were concerned. Heavy cavalry might find themselves on outpost duty, as did Le Marchant's Heavy Cavalry Brigade during the siege of Ciudad Rodrigo, while the Light might execute a fierce charge as they did at the cavalry combat at Villa-Garcia. The heavy cavalry tended to be larger men on larger horses and to carry heavier weapons, but unlike the French cuirassiers wore no body armour; in theory they were better suited for shock action on the field of battle, while the nimbler and more agile light horsemen might be expected to excel at outpost duty, patrolling and the pursuit. Wellington himself paid little attention to such niceties, using regiments as convenient without much regard for their official classification.

The heavy cavalryman went into action with a cut-down version of the Brown Bess musket, labelled a carbine, which has a barrel twenty-six inches long; his main weapon was a long, heavy, badly balanced sword, according to some critics the worst weapon ever issued to the British Army. The light cavalryman was also armed with a carbine, the Paget, which had an exceptionally short barrel, only sixteen inches, but again his main weapon was his sabre about thirty-three inches long and reputedly a light and handy weapon.

Officers carried a similar pattern sword to that of their men, and all ranks carried pistols. It was in their uniforms that the two types of cavalrymen differed most distinctly. Historically, the regular cavalry had developed from regiments of dragoons and in origin the dragoon had been little more than an infantryman on horseback. Marlborough, however, believed in shock action and the sword, limiting his cavalrymen to no more than three or four rounds for their carbines in battle, and this view had become generally accepted. The heavy cavalry regiments, still called dragoons or, more grandiosely, dragoon guards, however, retained in their uniform their old infantry connection, and at the beginning of the war were attired in red coats and white breeches. The light cavalry, light dragoons or more rarely, hussars, by now had totally renounced their origin. The colour of their jackets was basically blue, but became so adorned with wonderful and exotic additions that the modern Paris fashions would have had little to offer the well-dressed light dragoon.

But here the differences largely ended; neither in drills nor in composition does there appear to have been any great distinction; however, a marked difference soon developed between cavalry and infantry. Cavalry regiments had no battalions or depots, and were responsible for recruiting and training their own men; in addition, with their imposing chargers and cutting swords that could wound but seldom kill, they were far better at controlling riotous mobs than the infantry with their deadlier firearms and vicious bayonets that could be used only for the far more lethal thrust. Since the free-born Briton of the day was accustomed to voicing his views with no little force, the government made a habit of keeping a number of cavalry regiments in the country to help enforce its less popular decrees. For these reasons, cavalry regiments serving in the Peninsula normally left behind two troops to form a depot, going overseas with only eight, and later some regiments left behind four.

When the 10th Royal Hussars left England to join Wellington for his campaign of 1813, four troops under a major were sent to York to form a depot and keep an eye on the local populace, while according to its official history the regiment embarked six troops strong, with the following:

Hussars charging French cavalry. The metal chin-straps shown here are unusual. The pelisses are slung over the left shoulder to free the sword arm, but even so it was a common criticism that the coats were cut too tight in the arm. Plumes are not worn in the headdress; these were generally preserved for the less exacting conditions of ceremonial parades

lieutenant-colonels – 1; majors – 1; staff officers – 4 (presumably these were officers in regimental headquarters and included the adjutant, the quartermaster, and perhaps a doctor and veterinary surgeon); captains – 6; subalterns – 12; assistant adjutant – 1; regimental sergeant-major – 1; troop quartermasters – 2; troop sergeant-majors – 4; sergeants – 29; corporals – 24; trumpeters – 6; privates – 513; troop horses – 523. It is interesting to note that troop sergeant-majors appear to have begun to take over from troop quartermasters.

Although the regiment had only six troops, with about 580 rank and file, it was considerably stronger than many of the eight-troop regiments serving in the Peninsula at this time. Here the strength of most regiments fluctuated between 400 and 500; a number were considerably less. Yet in 1809 some of the cavalry regiments serving under Sir John Moore had mustered as many as 750 men. Even allowing for the wastage to be expected on service, it seems clear that the smaller regiments had proved more effective in the field.

On operations, no doubt for what must have appeared at that time good reason, the troop organization was almost entirely abandoned; troops worked in pairs to form squadrons under the senior troop commanders, and, curiously, the half-squadron, not the troop, was the basic subunit for manoeuvre. Captain Neville, in his treatise on light cavalry which was largely embodied in the cavalry manual of 1803, put forward the view that thirty-six or forty-eight files (i.e. seventy-two or ninety-six men and horses) composed a manageable squadron. This suggests that an eight troop regiment organized in four squadrons was at its best with under 400 men present in the ranks.

To adopt the operational organization troops first paraded and sized; then each pair of troops came together to form a squadron in a two-rank

Sabugal on the River Coa. (St Clair). A light cavalry outpost. The hussars are wearing their fur pelisses buttoned up. A dragoon in his helmet with a flowing mane sits on a log with two comrades wearing some strange headgear of their own. The men butchering the sheep are probably Portuguese light cavalry

line with the largest men from both in the centre; when in line the men on the flanks tended to lean inwards setting up a considerable pressure on the centre, and for this reason the heaviest men were placed there to prevent them being forced out of the ranks like corks from bottles of champagne. It seems unlikely that during operations this clumsy procedure was always followed, and in an emergency squadrons must surely have fallen in as such.

The intervals to be observed within the squadron were carefully defined. Between the front and rear ranks there was to be a horse's length; men in close order rode with their boot tops touching; in loose files boot tops were to be six inches apart, and in open files there was an interval of a horse's length between every man. When the squadron had been formed and the men had checked their dressing on the centre file, they were numbered and detailed into half-squadrons, quarter-squadrons and threes; (as in the infantry

the nomenclature was somewhat haphazard and such phrases as divisions and sub-divisions were occasionally used).

The numbering in threes was important. The space taken by a horse in the ranks was reckoned at three feet, or a third of a horse's length. Hence if every three men in a rank wheeled their horses independently to the right, the rank would face in that direction in column of threes with a horse's length between each three. It would then be in a very manageable formation, and when it had reached its new position, on the command 'front' the men could wheel to the left and, since there was a horse's length between each three, could resume line without falling into disorder. In a squadron both ranks would perform this manoeuvre simultaneously, the rear rank wheeling up beside their opposite numbers in the front rank and the whole squadron facing to the right or left in a column of sixes. (The drill was in practice a little more complex than that outlined here, as it involved men reining back.) Movement by threes was normally used for all changes of formation. In true British style, when the order 'threes about' was given, in fact the squadron moved on a front of six men.

For movement over any distance, it was recommended that regiments should move in column of half-squadrons, or if this was impossible, by threes (i.e. sixes) or as a last resort in file or single file. The principle was that wherever feasible the length of the regimental column should not exceed that of the regiment in line.

As in the infantry, the main battle formations were columns of half-squadrons or squadrons, and line. In line, owing to the peril of pressure developing on the centre, an interval was preserved between squadrons, and in an advance the men in each aligned themselves on the centre file of their own particular squadron; the squadron leader himself rode a horse's length in front of his centre man and therefore could control the pace and direction of the whole squadron; to ensure that the regiment preserved its line the squadron leaders of the flank squadrons aligned themselves on those in the centre, while these in turn took their positions from the commanding officer who gallantly rode in the centre of his regiment a horse's length in front of the rank of squadron leaders, a rather more hazardous position than that occupied by the infantry colonel happily ensconced six paces behind his colours. Of the remaining officers and sergeants in the squadron, an officer, covered by a sergeant took post on each of its flanks, three sergeants occupied positions on the right of quarter-squadrons, and the rest made up a serre-file, or supernumerary rank, a horse's length behind the rear rank. The trumpeter or trumpeters, rode in the serre-file, but directly behind the squadron leader. Commands were initially given by word of mouth, generally repeated by the appropriate call on the trumpet; the most important calls such as 'charge' or 'rally' were taken up by all the trumpeters. Bugles were sometimes used instead of trumpets, but the manual of 1803 clearly thought this was a deplorable surrender to utility. It stated of the bugle horn: 'Soundings are exactly the same as those for the trumpet in place of which the bugle horn may occasionally be substituted. The trumpet is always to be considered as the principal musical instrument for the sounding; it particularly belongs to the line and the bugle horn to detached parties.'

The main cavalry method of attack was the charge. On this subject the manual of 1803 stated, 'When cavalry attack cavalry, the squadrons must be firm and compact; when they attack infantry the files may be opened; when they attack a battery, they must not ride up in front of it, but they must in two divisions attack on each flank, the files opened.'

'When cavalry attack infantry they should in general do it in column; the squadrons of the column should have at least three times as much distance between them as the extent of their front. The leading squadron, after breaking the enemy's line should move forward and form, the two succeeding ones should wheel outwards by half squadrons and charge along the line.' The action after a charge was important, the manual continues, 'In a charge of either infantry or cavalry the instant the enemy gives way the line must again be formed and the pursuit continued by light troops.' This was easy enough to lay down, but it was a ruling all too often forgotten in practice. Time and again the British cavalry failed to rally after a successful charge, galloping off in a wild pursuit of their beaten enemy, only to be confronted when horses were blown by fresh French cavalry and their triumph to be turned into disaster.

In a charge against infantry, the gallop began about 300 yards away to cut to a minimum the time under fire; against cavalry, on the other hand, the most important consideration was to arrive with reasonably fresh horses for the mêlée, and only the last 150 yards were covered at a gallop. It is difficult to believe that two squadrons ever galloped at each other in a compact mass. If they did so they would have resembled two motorists driving along the crown of the road and colliding with a closing speed of thirty miles an hour, and the drivers would have been in a much happier position than the cavalryman on his horse. Colonel Tomkinson, who served throughout the Peninsular War in the 16th Light Dragoons, made some illuminating comments when describing a skirmish:

Captain Belli's squadron with one of the Hussars, was in advance; and the enemy having sent forward two or three squadrons, Major Myers attempted to oppose them in front of a defile. He waited so long and was so indecisive, and the enemy coming up so close, that he ordered the squadron of the 16th to charge. The enemy's squadron was about twice their strength and waited their charge.

This is the first instance I ever met with two bodies of cavalry coming into opposition, and both standing, as invariably as I have observed it, one or the other runs away.

Our men rode up and began sabring, but were so outnumbered that they could do nothing and were obliged to retire across the defile in confusion, the enemy having brought up more troops to that point.

The ability to outflank an enemy was clearly one of the keys to a successful cavalry action and the length of front was of critical importance. The manual specified, 'Two or three squadrons in attack may divide into small bodies with 14 or

Lieutenant-General Sir Stapleton Cotton. He is wearing the shako of a light dragoon and the epaulettes of a field officer. He must be wearing the uniform of the colonel of a regiment

16 files in each and intervals between them equal to their front, the second or reserve covering the intervals 150 yards to the rear; if only two squadrons, the first line should be four small troops, the second of two again sub-divided, three covering the intervals and one outflanking.' The use of the word 'troop' here illustrates the remarkably casual attitude to terminology typical of the period.

In the rugged country of the Portuguese border and of much of Spain, the cavalry had few opportunities to exert a decisive influence in battle. Their most valuable functions were to act as the eyes and ears of the army and to screen it in movement and at rest. Single well-mounted sentries called vedettes could observe and hang around an enemy and gallop away if threatened. The tactics of the cavalry when patrolling or on outpost were strikingly similar to those of the light infantry. They worked in pairs in open order, covering each other and using their carbines to fire from the saddle – apart from the difficulty of persuading their horses to stand still

Firing from the saddle. The uniform is that of a former period. The horse seems to be rearing, perhaps to register a protest at the odd happenings over his head

The Battle of Salamanca, 1812. Le Marchant's heavy brigade making the charge that broke the French infantry. Both the infantry and cavalry uniforms shown are those of ceremonial parades and not service where overalls had replaced breeches. In particular the cocked hat of the cavalrymen had proved useless on service, and until it was replaced by a helmet the troopers generally wore forage caps

while aiming and firing, reloading must have presented nearly insuperable problems and one suspects that the effect of such fire was moral rather than physical.

The standard cavalry formation was the brigade composed of two, three or, less usually, four regiments. During the early stages of the war Wellington formed two cavalry divisions; although these on occasion consisted of two brigades, one heavy, one light, their organization was far more fluid than that of the infantry and tended to reflect the needs of a particular situation. He was plagued by incompetent divisional commanders, and from 1812 onwards discarded the divisional organization, leaving the cavalry brigades largely independent under the general direction of a single cavalry commander, General Sir Stapleton Cotton, who normally exercised control from army headquarters.

For most of the war Wellington was heavily outnumbered in cavalry by the French; during the first three years he had only eight regiments, but towards the end of 1811 matters improved; during the Salamanca campaign of 1812 he had sixteen, and used his new-found strength to decisive advantage at the Battle of Salamanca; here Le Marchant, with a Heavy Cavalry Brigade, in brilliant charge shattered a tottering French line to turn a French reverse into utter defeat.

The following year at Vitoria and during the battles in the Pyrenees the country inhibited the use of large bodies of horsemen. However, during Wellington's great advance through Spain to the borders of France the cavalry faithfully imposed an impenetrable screen in front of his armies and enabled him utterly to deceive the French commanders.

Artillery

The organization of the Royal Artillery reflected the somewhat casual fashion in which that arm had evolved; it had a logic all its own. Gunners were men who fired guns; guns were tubes down which various types of projectiles could be stuffed to be subsequently blown to a remote destination. The process clearly required certain specialized skills not to be found in the infantry, but since one tube, give or take a few feet in length and a few inches in diameter, much resembled another, a man who could deal with one manifestly could deal with another. It would be a false and expensive move, therefore, to train gunners to deal with only one particular type of equipment; what was needed was a number of all-purpose gunners capable of firing any type of cannon that might be appropriate to the task of the moment.

At the beginning of the eighteenth century, when it had become clear that artillery was likely to be a permanent feature of the battle-field, the British Army raised a Regiment of Artillery consisting of a single battalion. The old Roman organization of tens and centuries which seemed to work well enough for the infantry was obviously equally suitable for gunners. When over the years more battalions were raised they were composed of ten companies each about a hundred strong. These companies were expected to man any type of cannon, so there seemed little point in issuing them with a standard number of guns, or indeed any guns at all. When the need arose a battery of guns could be drawn from the gun-park, the number and type being those deemed suitable for the particular task. Since it might

Royal Horse Artillery changing position at speed. The gun detachments normally rode separately as outriders. Presumably in this incident it has not proved possible to bring forward their horses. A field officer of the Royal Foot Artillery seems to be enquiring about the move

1 General, review order, 1814
2 Staff Officer, service dress, 1814
3 Ensign, 9th or East Norfolk
  Regiment of Foot, service dress, 1814

MICHAEL ROFFE

A

1 **Field Officer, 7th Foot (Royal Fusiliers), full dress, 1813**

2 **Infantry Officer, Line Regiment, cold weather uniform, 1812**

3 **Private, 3rd or East Kent Regiment of Foot (Buffs), marching order, 1814**

MICHAEL ROFFE

1 Rifleman, 95th Foot (The Rifle
  Brigade), service dress, 1811
2 Portuguese Rifleman, 5th Cacadores,
  campaign dress, 1811
3 Corporal, Portuguese 8th Infantry,
  full dress, 1810

MICHAEL ROFFE

C

1 Corporal, Grenadier Company,
   42nd of Foot (Royal Highland
   Regiment or Black Watch),
   service dress, 1810
2 Officer, 52nd Light Infantry,
   service dress, 1814
3 Colour Sergeant, 11th Foot,
   full dress, August 1813

MICHAEL ROFFE

D

**Private, 10th (Prince of Wales's Own Royal)
Regiment of Light Dragoons (Hussars), campaign dress, 1814**

MICHAEL ROFFE

E

1 **Officer, 9th Light Dragoons,
   parade dress, 1812**
2 **Private, 3rd Dragoon Guards,
   service dress, 1814**
3 **Gunner, Royal Horse Artillery,
   service dress, 1810**

MICHAEL ROFFE

F

1 Officer, Marching Battalion,
  Royal Artillery, service dress, 1814
2 Gunner, Royal Artillery,
  service dress, 1810
3 Sapper, Royal Sappers
  and Miners, service dress, 1814

MICHAEL ROFFE

G

1 **Field Officer, Royal Engineers,**
  service dress, 1811
2 **Pioneer, Line Regiment,**
  29th Foot, service dress, 1811
3 **Drum Major, 57th Foot,**
  ceremonial dress, 1812

MICHAEL ROFFE

H

prove unnecessary to move the guns it would be folly to provide any form of transport. The infantry humped their muskets, there seemed no reason why the gunners should not pull their guns; if transport should be necessary, the sensible answer was to hire contractors for the occasion and discharge them when the occasion was over.

It was a delightfully simple approach and one likely to appeal strongly to those in financial authority. The possibility that, while it might provide the cheapest form of artillery, the system was hardly likely to produce the most efficient, was only slowly and reluctantly accepted. The first reform came when some astute member of the Board of Ordnance, which controlled such matters, realized that invalid companies were quite fit enough to man the guns on permanent fortifications, and thus the first tentative attempt at specialization was introduced. This reform, being an economy, was relatively painless. But the next, the decision to discontinue the hiring of civilian contractors to transport guns, was another matter. Yet civilian transport had indisputable disadvantages. Civilians, for some inscrutable reason of their own, were very apt to depart from the battle-field at the most critical moments, leaving the guns stranded or without ammunition. As these civilians were not subject to military law, the only punishment was to discharge them, a service that they had frequently already performed for themselves. By the time of the Peninsular War, however, a Corps of Royal Artillery Drivers had been raised, but this corps was completely separate from the Royal Regiment of Artillery and was commanded by officers from the Commissary. It was organized in troops from which drivers and horses were allotted to the artillery companies as might be necessary. This was the organization in force in the Peninsula. When a company of artillery had been allotted a battery of guns and the wherewithal to move them, it was known as a 'Brigade of Artillery'. This term, which had a completely different significance for most of the first half of this century, may be confusing; since these brigades corresponded to what in modern parlance would be called a field battery, it will, perhaps, be less confusing to use this title.

In the early days of the Peninsular War the finding of the gunners from one source and transport and guns from others had the unfortunate results to be expected; in particular the gunners tended to suffer from a critical shortage of transport. However with the passage of time the artillery companies operated for long periods with a particular type of gun and a roughly standardized amount of transport, but even then a company might find itself suddenly drafted to man siege guns, and the provision of horses and drivers to make the guns mobile still had its problems. In 1813 Captain Cairns commanding an artillery company wrote, as quoted in the Dickson papers:

We, that is our brigade [i.e. battery] and the Household Cavalry, arrived here on the 27th. Although marching with them we are not in their brigade; however, as we are of the Reserve, I am quite well pleased with them, as with no superior officers of our corps being now left to myself to forage and arrange as I please.

I am getting my naked drivers clothed here as well as I can. These lads were only three days in Lisbon, when they were pushed up to the Army and unluckily fell to my lot.

They leave England paid in advance, sell half their necessaries when lying at Portsmouth and the other half either at Lisbon or on the road, the driver officers never inspecting their kit. Thus they join a brigade perfectly naked. In my establishment of 100 drivers, I have men from three different Troops. I am resolved to

Royal Artillery Drivers. They wore blue jackets with red facings and the same pattern helmet as the Royal Horse Artillery. The non-commissioned-officer is in full dress with yellow braid and velvet trimmings. The man on the wagon is in undress uniform and wearing a forage cap and stable jacket. Artillery drivers carried no personal weapons

see that my officer of drivers, Lieutenant Dalton, does his duty in supplying them with necessaries, soap and salt. That is all I allow him to interfere with. My own officers look to the stable duties, and inspect the drivers' kits of their division every Saturday. The poor drivers are sadly to be pitied – considering the labour of taking care of two horses and harness they are worse paid than any other troops, and when left to the management of their own officers they are luckless indeed. By being with a brigade there is some hope of instilling into them the idea that they are soldiers.

The first part of this letter indicates another curious aspect of the artillery organization. At any one time an artillery battalion might have its companies spread as far apart as the West Indies, Spain and Sicily. All attempts to concentrate battalions in particular regions invariably failed and the commanding officers, accepting with philosophy the impossibility of visiting their companies, generally stayed in Woolwich, contenting themselves with organizing drafts and looking after the administration of their companies overseas. In consequence there tended to be no real gunner hierarchy with the armies in the field. In operations near England, such as that at Walcheren, a reasonable number of senior officers might take part, but farther afield there was often only one senior artillery officer, perhaps a major, who acted as the Commander Royal Artillery, and his duties rarely extended to more than solving the many administrative problems which the peculiar gunner organization was likely to produce. The artillery company commanders were virtually independent, and as Cairns's letter shows, they were probably far from dissatisfied with their fate.

In the Peninsula the artillery initially was officially in charge of a Major-General, Royal Artillery. He seldom accompanied the army in the field, partly because his most important duties were administrative, partly because Wellington seems to have taken a dislike to the two generals who successively occupied the post. During most of the war he took as his artillery adviser Major Alexander Dickson (later Major-General Sir Alexander Dickson) a captain in the Royal

Artillery who had transferred to the Portuguese service to obtain a step in rank. It was a fortunate choice, and quite possibly Wellington was happy to have as his artillery adviser an officer too junior to press on him gratuitous advice, something he detested. During the course of the war, Dickson was promoted Lieutenant-Colonel and in 1813 was appointed to command all the artillery in the field. By the time of the Battle of Vitoria he had accumulated the nucleus of a staff and majors were to be found on occasion co-ordinating the activities of two or more batteries.

This lack of a gunner hierarchy, particularly during the early period, may have influenced Wellington against using his artillery massed. He allotted one battery semi-permanently to each division and that battery rarely strayed far from its parent formation. The reserve artillery was generally minimal in strength and artillery tactics seldom rose above the level of the battery. At this level the standard became remarkably high.

But although the company of Royal Foot Artillery in the Peninsula remained a maid-of-all-work,

Sir Alexander Dickson wearing a post-Napoleonic uniform. He has the Army gold cross with a number of Peninsular clasps

the first step in producing a battery trained and equipped for the field had already been taken. On 1 January 1793 orders were issued for the formation of A and B Troops Royal Horse Artillery. These Troops were designed to act with the cavalry, and, therefore, had to be highly mobile, fast into action and quick and accurate in their shooting. They were trained almost exclusively in their own particular role, and their drivers, although initially drawn from the Corps of Royal Artillery Drivers, were carried on the Troop strength and to all intents and purposes formed an integral part of the unit. Only officers of proven ability and the pick of the recruits were posted in. As a result these troops soon established a very high reputation. Since they supported the cavalry, they adopted a light cavalry style of uniform quite different from that of their comrades with the infantry. Troops R.H.A. supported the two cavalry divisions in the Peninsula and that most famous of divisions, the Light Division.

In an embarkation return dated 8 June 1809 quoted in Captain Duncan's *History of the Royal Artillery*, Captain Ross's Troop R.H.A. is shown as being composed as follows:

Captains	2
Subalterns	3
Assistant Surgeons	1
N.C.O.s	13
Trumpeters	1
Artificers	7
Gunners	81
Drivers	54
Total	162
Horses	162
6-pounder guns	5
$5\frac{1}{2}$ in. Howitzers	1
Ammunition wagons	6
Baggage wagons	3

This shows a troop R.H.A. at full strength. Whether horse or field, batteries were commanded by captains with 'second captains' to understudy them. The light six-pounders and the howitzer were generally drawn by teams of six horses, but for the wagons mules might be substituted. Gunners carried sabres but the drivers

were unarmed. During the campaigns the R.H.A. fully justified their position as the right of the line, and at the Battle of Fuentes de Onoro under Captain Ramsay, their second captain, Bull's Troop R.H.A. performed a famous feat. The Troop was cut off by French cavalry and was given up for lost by the remainder of the army. Ramsay however, limbered up his guns and charged the French cavalry at the gallop. The gunners broke through the astonished French horsemen and rejoined the Army with their guns intact.

The work of the Companies Royal Foot Artillery, although less glamorous, was no less vital to the success of British arms. Since their guns were heavier than those of the horse artillery, these companies had rather more gunners on establishment. In the Dickson papers a company was shown with an authorized establishment of 2 captains, 3 subalterns, 4 sergeants, 4 corporals, 9 bombardiers, 120 gunners and 3 drummers, giving a total of 145 all ranks. In the field, its strength probably fluctuated between 110 and 130. The battery was armed with five field guns, 9-pounders or heavy 6-pounders, and one $5\frac{1}{2}$ inch howitzer. In addition it might have allotted to it about 100 drivers and horses and mules totalling altogether nearly 200. Teams of eight horses harnessed in pairs were normally used to drag the guns, but for the ammunition and baggage (a standard field battery might have eight ammunition and three baggage wagons plus a travelling forge) mules were often employed. However, the companies were far from standardized and would reflect in their organization the prejudices of their company commanders, or the needs of a particular task. The drivers would have a commissary officer theoretically in charge of them, and being mounted and therefore unable to understand drum calls, had their own trumpeter.

The characteristics of the guns in both field batteries and the Horse Artillery troops differed little, those in the horse artillery being merely lighter for greater speed of movement. There were three main types of projectile, roundshot, grape and shell. Round shot was a solid iron ball that had an extreme effective range of about 1,200 yards. It depended for its effect on the velocity with which it struck its target, hence field guns

The passage of the River Douro by Murray's Division, 1809 (St Clair). In the foreground foot artillerymen have taken the barrel of a field gun, probably a heavy six-pounder, off its carriage preparatory to embarkation – the triangular ornaments on the back of the gunners' coatees show up clearly. Behind them a light dragoon who has left his carbine on his horse is having trouble coaxing it into the boat, while on the left an infantry sergeant, clutching his spontoon, superintends the embarkation of his men

needed long, heavy barrels to stand up to large charges and impart a high muzzle velocity. On the other hand, since these barrels had to be mounted on robust yet light carriages that could travel across country unharmed and at a reasonable speed, the weight of the barrel had to be severely limited; British field pieces initially only took a six lb. ball, not a very daunting missile, and later a model was introduced capable of firing one of nine lb.

Roundshot, unless striking a column of troops, was comparatively harmless, but it was the only missile that could be used against a moving target at ranges of over 300 yards. Under this distance grape was far more effective. This name was applied indiscriminately to grapeshot itself, canister and case. Grapeshot consisted of about nine iron balls sewn together in a canvas bag that dissolved after the rounds left the gun, and

received its title from its resemblance to an oversize bunch of grapes; it was issued only to the eighteen-pounder and twenty-four-pounder guns of the siege train. Case and canister, as the names imply, were metal containers filled with a hundred small bullets or forty large ones. The container disintegrated as the round left the muzzle and the shot fanned out to produce a deadly pattern of destruction for a distance of nearly 300 yards.

Between 300 and 1,000 yards shells could be very effective, but only if the target was reasonably stationary. The common shell, as it was called, consisted of a hollow iron ball containing a fuze and a bursting charge. The fuze was ignited by the explosion of the charge that propelled the shell, and if all went well, it would cause the bursting charge to explode after the shell had landed; fragments of the exploding shell case would, it was hoped, strike anyone rash enough to be standing near by. To achieve this desirable result it was necessary that the shell should have thin walls and carry a large bursting charge, so that the casing broke up into numerous fragments moving with a lethal velocity; in consequence the shell was too large and too fragile to be fired from a field gun. However the shell did not need to be given the high muzzle velocity of roundshot and a shorter, lighter piece could be used. The $5\frac{1}{2}$ inch howitzer, the standard field piece for firing shells, although capable of accommodating a 24 lb. ball, owing to its light construction and short barrel (only 33 inches compared with 72 inches for the light 6-pounder, 96 inches for the heavy, and 84 inches for the 9-pounder) could keep up even with the cavalry.

Since field guns could not fire shells, every battery included a howitzer. This complicated arrangements for ammunition, and experiments were made with all-howitzer batteries, but these proved too specialized to suit the dispersed way in which Wellington generally deployed his guns.

There was an obvious need to make field guns more effective at ranges over 300 yards and Lieutenant Shrapnel developed a shell originally called spherical case, but which later attained more fame under the name of its inventor. He filled his shell with bullets; now the bursting charge had only to be strong enough to break open the shell case and let loose the bullets, it could be much reduced and the walls of the shell could be thicker. Spherical case was issued to all field guns, although technical difficulties prevented its being fully effective at that time.

In a regimental order the following proportions

A $5\frac{1}{2}$-inch howitzer

were laid down for a hundred rounds. Field guns were to carry 60 rounds roundshot, 30 of spherical case and 10 of common case; howitzers 50 rounds spherical case, 10 rounds common case and 40 rounds common shell. Ammunition was to be carried at the scale of 180 rounds per 6-pounder gun, 116 per 9-pounder and 84 per howitzer.

In action guns were aimed by lining up the barrel with the target, hence the gun-layer for either field guns or howitzers had to have a clear view of his target. Range was obtained by elevating the barrel, but even with howitzers it was rare to elevate it more than 10° with the horizontal.

To load the gun, first a charge of gunpowder was rammed down the barrel, then the missile, and finally some wadding to keep it in place. At the same time powder was trickled down a vent which led to the charge, or some combustible material was inserted. When the order to fire was given, a slow match or port-fire was applied to this powder which burnt down to the charge and caused it to explode. Immediately after firing, the gun barrel had to be sponged out to remove any burning embers that might remain and prematurely ignite the next charge; if for any reason a sponge was not available the gun was out of action. Five or six men were sufficient to load and point a gun but four or five more were needed to prepare the ammunition and help haul it back to its firing position, as the shock of each discharge would cause it to recoil a few feet. Rates of fire are not known for certain. General B.P. Hughes, perhaps the best authority on the subject, calculated that under battle conditions guns could probably fire two rounds of roundshot or three of grape in a minute. Dickson merely observed that the rate of fire for howitzers was slower than that for guns: it may be guessed at about three rounds in two minutes.

Besides the field artillery there were two more categories in the Peninsula, the siege train, which will be considered later, and rockets. Although in the Peninsula no complete battery of rockets ever operated, as Wellington viewed their uncertain behaviour with considerable distaste, it is recorded that 'Captain Lane's rocket detachment did good service during the crossing of the R. Adour before the battle of Orthes.'

Wellington's handling of his artillery has sometimes been called in question, yet his method corresponded exactly to his own particular tactical policy. Napoleon concentrated his artillery and signalled his attacks by massive bombardments. Wellington, generally fighting on the defensive, was determined to conceal his dispositions until the last possible moment; he therefore spread his artillery across his front, placing the batteries under the control of his divisional commanders, so that it was possible for the commander on the spot to use his guns to best advantage without the hampering rigidity inevitable under a system of centralized control. Concentrations of artillery might indeed pave the way for a successful attack, but in defence it could result in furnishing an easy target for the guns of the enemy and might rob an area of vitally needed artillery support.

At the same time Wellington was quite competent to deploy his individual batteries to best advantage himself. At the battle of Salamanca the French had a considerable superiority in artillery, but it was the British guns that exercised the most influence on the battle. During the initial attack on the French flank, they were positioned at right angles to the infantry line of advance and raked the front of the French columns with deadly effect. When later in the battle Clausel launched a counter-attack that achieved a considerable initial success, the French infantry found themselves advancing up a shallow valley with the British artillery, personally posted by Wellington long before, pouring in a devastating cross-fire from the high ground on either side, a fire which contributed powerfully to their eventual repulse. It was perhaps natural for the Royal Artillery to watch enviously Napoleon's technique for handling guns *en masse*, a technique perfectly suited to the tactics he used. It did not follow that Wellington's less ostentatious use of that arm was any less well suited to the tactics that at Waterloo led to the defeat of the Emperor of the French.

Badajoz. The 3rd Division takes the Castle by escalade. A bare-headed field officer, probably Major Ridge of the 5th, is stepping on to the ramparts while a grenadier waves his comrades forward

Sieges and Sappers

The organization of the Royal Artillery may have seemed peculiar, but the organization of the Royal Engineers had the distinction of being barely discernible. For most of the eighteenth century, like the inmates of a college at a university with fellows and dons but no undergraduates, Royal Engineer officers were unencumbered by the presence of soldiers. They moved in the aura of a mysterious craft no lesser mortals could comprehend, and depended on contract labour for the execution of their designs.

However, after the capture of Gibraltar it was realized that contract labour might not relish repairing fortifications while a siege was actually in progress, and a company of military artificers was raised for this purpose. Later, when revolutionary France threatened invasion, new companies under Engineer officers were formed to fortify the English coastline and the name was changed to the Corps of Royal Military Artificers.

But this corps remained distinct from the Royal Engineers and at the time of the Peninsular War Engineer officers still had virtually no troops under their command; in addition, although they were competent enough in the art of fortification, as they showed when constructing the Lines of Torres Vedras, they had no experience and little knowledge of how to conduct a siege. Since sieges were considered pre-eminently the province of the Engineer assisted by the Artilleryman, being clearly too complicated for the ordinary army officer to understand, the inexperience of the engineers, and above all the lack of trained engineer units was to cost the Peninsular Army very dear. The tragedy was the greater in that during the eighteenth century an elaborate ritual had developed by which a siege, if the attackers had sufficient men and siege guns, became largely a formal and relatively bloodless exercise in excavation and mathematics. General Jones, who as a young engineer officer was present at all Wellington's major sieges, has described the accepted procedure: the besiegers broke ground about 700 yards from the ramparts of the fortress:

This is effected by secretly approaching the place in the night with a body of men carrying entrenching tools and the remainder armed. The former dig a trench in the ground parallel to the fortifications to be attacked, whilst those with arms remain in readiness to protect those at work should the garrison sally out. During the night this trench is made of sufficient extent to cover from the missiles of the place the number of men requisite to cope with the garrison . . . This trench is afterwards progressively widened and deepened till it forms a covered road called a parallel, and along this road guns, wagons and men can securely move equally sheltered from the view and the missiles of the garrison. Batteries of guns and mortars are then constructed on the side of the road next the garrison and in a short time by superiority of fire silence all those [enemy guns] which bear on the works of the attack.

The procedure was continued at distances progressively nearer the enemy and from about 500 yards onwards heavy guns using groundshot would start to batter a gap, called a breach, in the ramparts of the fortress. While the guns demolished a selected section of the wall the mortars had an important task to perform. They resembled stocky wide-mouthed howitzers with barrels permanently set at an angle of forty-five degrees: their role was to lob large bombs into or over the fixed defences of the enemy subduing their fire and enabling the construction of the parallels and the covered road to proceed until the covered road led into the breach itself. At this juncture it was customary for the garrison to admit defeat and walk out with the 'honours of war'. If properly carried out, time and gunpowder were consumed rather than lives.

The main difficulty arose when the approaches came within 300 yards of the enemy ramparts. Jones continues:

Then the work becomes truly hazardous and can only be performed by selected brave men who have acquired a difficult and most dangerous art called sapping from which they themselves are styled sappers. An indispensable auxiliary to the sapper is the miner, the exercise of whose art requires an even greater degree of skill, courage, and conduct, than that of his principal. The duty of the miner at a siege is to accompany the sapper, to listen for and discover the enemy's miner at work underground, and prevent his blowing up the head of the road either by sinking down and meeting him, when a subterranean conflict ensues, or by running a gallery close to his opponent and forcing him to quit his work by means of suffocating compositions and a thousand arts of chicanery, the knowledge of which he has acquired from experience. Sappers would be unable of themselves, without the aid of skilful miners, to execute that part of the covered road forming the descent into the ditch, and in various other portions of the road, the assistance of the miner is indispensable to the sapper; indeed without their joint labours and steady co-operation no besieger's approaches ever reached the walls of a fortress. A siege, scientifically prosecuted, though it calls for the greatest personal bravery, the greatest exertion and extraordinary labour in all employed, is beautifully certain in its progress and result.

Unhappily this was never true of the British sieges in the Peninsula. Wellington had neither the trained sappers to accomplish the final stages of the siege, nor sufficient guns to silence those of the enemy; he always lacked time. In consequence he was forced to storm imperfectly blasted breaches from too far away. Even if he was successful the cost of life, as at Badajoz, could be appalling, while he frequently risked a bloody repulse, as at Burgos and San Sebastian.

The number of trained engineers at his sieges is revealing. At the unsuccessful attempt on Badajoz in 1811 he had seventeen engineer officers distributed at two per brigade, excluding

The siege of Ciudad Rodrigo. On 19 January 1812 the French garrison made a sally while the covering troops were being relieved, and nearly captured the breaching batteries. Here the working party are seen putting up a stout resistance with anything that came to hand

The Kurnool Mortar

the commander in charge of the siege. He had besides twenty-five men of the Royal Corps of Military Artificers who were no more than storekeepers responsible for the engineer park and the issue of engineer stores. He formed an *ad hoc* engineer unit by calling in forty-eight carpenters and forty-eight miners from his infantry battalions. At the sieges of Ciudad Rodrigo and Badajoz in 1812 his engineer resources were much the same and he supplemented them with twelve officers and 180 men culled again from the infantry, but these were no substitute for properly trained men.

After the atrocious number of casualties he suffered at the storm of Badajoz, he wrote home bitterly complaining of the lack of trained sappers, and Horse Guards responded by creating the Royal Corps of Sappers and Miners. At the siege of San Sebastian he had 105 rank and file from the newly-formed corps, but their numbers were quite inadequate and the fortress fell only after the second attempt at a storm.

Guns were the other half of the siege equation. Siege guns were heavy and difficult to move, requiring long trains of oxen if they travelled by

An artillery officer personally lays a siege gun while two others stand ready to observe the fall of shot. The artilleryman with the handspike wears two fringed epaulettes and is therefore a corporal (bombardiers, equivalent to the modern lance corporal, wore only one fringe on the right shoulder). Chevrons, although officially adopted by the Royal Artillery in 1802 to conform with the infantry, were not actually worn until 1813

road. The siege train sent out from England for the siege of Ciudad Rodrigo is fairly typical. Jones quotes this as being:

24-pounders iron	32
18-pounders ,,	4
10 inch mortars iron	8
$5\frac{1}{2}$ inch mortars ,,	20
$5\frac{1}{2}$ inch mortars brass	10
8 inch howitzers ,,	2

However, for various reasons only thirty-eight of these were actually used at the siege and to man them there were 171 British gunners and 371 Portuguese, giving a total of 542 non-commissioned-officers and men; of these, Jones noted, '85 men over two reliefs for laboratory and magazine duties and escorts and to replace casualties'. The actual gun detachments were only six men strong; this may seem strangely small, but the guns were aimed with a deliberation that was almost pedantic, and care had to be taken to avoid overheating the barrels; as a result rates of fire as compared with field guns were slow. At San Sebastian a breaching battery of ten guns fired 350 rounds per gun over a period of $15\frac{1}{2}$ hours, giving an overall average of a little more than one round per gun every three minutes. Jones said of this, 'such a rate of firing was probably never equalled at any siege'.

As regards supplies and the movement of stores there was a small British unit, 'the Royal Waggon Train', but for most of his transport Wellington had to depend on locally engaged Spanish bullock carts and pack mules, and for rations on the local purchases of his commissary officers. Medical arrangements were rudimentary. Every regiment had its own surgeon, but there were no ambulances or field hospitals, and the sick and wounded were cared for, so far as they were cared for at all, in improvised hospitals set up at nearby towns.

The Royal Waggon Train. The coatee was blue with red facings and the cut of the jacket resembled that of the artillery drivers

Conclusion

It can be said with justice that despite its many anomalies the Peninsular Army under Wellington was probably one of the finest that the world has known. Clausewitz suggested that as a war progressed the best men in the armies engaged became casualties resulting in a general levelling of standards. This process almost certainly happened to the Napoleonic armies, but Wellington was always careful of the lives of his men, and in the later stages of the war he and his army together merited the somewhat abused title, invincible. He himself remarked that if he had had his old Peninsular Army under him at Waterloo, instead of the astonishing miscellany of nationalities with which he was presented, the issue would never have been in doubt and the whole affair ended in three hours. Finally, a point not to be forgotten, one third of that magnificent army was Portuguese, and when he came to confront Napoleon in Belgium, he tried to have some of his veteran Portuguese regiments sent to him, but he appealed in vain.

The Plates

A1 General, review order, 1814

The 'loops' (the technical term for the long, false button-holes) on the lapels, cuffs and tails of the coatee were spaced evenly for generals, in threes for lieutenant-generals, and in pairs for major-generals. Two gold epaulettes were worn until 1811, when they were replaced by a gold aiguillette on the left shoulder. The cocked hat and feather were worn as shown in review order, but on active service a lower version was worn fore-and-aft for greater convenience.

A2 Staff Officer, service dress, 1814

This officer is wearing the uniform of an assistant adjutant-general or an assistant quarter-master-general. The embroidered loops were distinctive of all staff officers below general rank. They were in silver for the A and Q staff, and gold for aides-de-camp. Deputy assistants and brigade majors also wore silver lace, with only one epaulette, worn on the right shoulder by infantry and on the left by cavalry. Brigade majors were usually captains in rank, but those who were regimental majors did not wear the two epaulettes of a major when in staff pattern uniform, as they would then have been wearing the uniform of the senior grade posts of assistant adjutant- or quarter-master-general.

A3 Ensign, 9th or East Norfolk Regiment of Foot, service dress, 1814

The ensign was the junior commissioned rank in the infantry, corresponding to the cornet of cavalry and the second lieutenant of artillery. He wears the so-called 'Belgic' shako, officially adopted in 1812; earlier pattern 'stovepipe' shakos remained in use until stocks were exhausted, however. The double-breasted coatee came into use at the turn of the century. The tails, originally long as in a civilian tail-coat, were gradually shortened for convenience. The coatee could be worn buttoned up, but usually the top three buttons were left undone and the lapels turned back to reveal the same facing colour as on the collar and cuffs. The ground of the Regimental Colour he carries is of the same facing colour.

B1 Field Officer, 7th Foot (Royal Fusiliers), full dress, 1813

Wings were worn on the shoulders by all ranks of the grenadier and light companies of infantry battalions, and by all companies of light infantry and fusilier regiments. The Royal Fusiliers have blue facings, a distinction of all 'Royal' regiments. Their fur 'grenadier' caps, and grenade skirt ornaments, were worn to mark the original connection of the Fusiliers with the artillery; they were formed to escort the artillery, being armed with the then new flintlock fusil. Field officers at this time wore two epaulettes, but company officers had one on the right shoulder only.

Grenadier and light company officers wore two lace wings, as did all officers of fusilier and light infantry regiments. Field officers of these regiments wore small epaulettes over their wings.

B2 Infantry Officer, Line Regiment, cold weather uniform, 1812

The stovepipe shako is protected by an oilskin cover with a flap at the neck. Other types of headdress, including the helmets of the cavalry, had similar covers adapted to their shape. The greatcoat is the approved dismounted version (although some officers had shorter, fur-trimmed coats, while others had very long patterns reaching almost to the ground). The crimson waist sash was the distinction of an officer, tied on the left by cavalry and all field officers, and on the right by dismounted and all company officers. The gorget was worn by officers of the battalion companies when on duty, attached to the collar of the coatee by a ribbon of the facing colour. Light infantry officers wore curved swords, as did most field officers; the remainder carried a narrow, straight sword.

B3 Private, 3rd or East Kent Regiment of Foot (Buffs), marching order, 1814

The 3rd of Foot took their ancient nickname from the buff facings of their coats. The 'Belgic' shako shown here was made of felt, and the plume was carried on the left-hand side to avoid confusion with the French when viewed from a distance. Grenadier companies had a white plume, light companies a green one, and the battalion companies the national colours of white and red. Grey trousers and spat gaiters were officially sanctioned for active service in 1811, replacing the white breeches and black gaiters previously worn. The shade of grey depended on the quality of material and the effects of weathering.

The Battle of Fuentes de Onoro, 5 May 1811 (St Clair). The regimental surgeons, wearing the cocked hat of battalion staff officers, have set up a regimental dressing station to which stretcher-bearers are carrying a wounded man on an improvised stretcher. The musicians in a regiment were normally trained to perform this duty

C1 Rifleman, 95th Foot (The Rifle Brigade), service dress, 1811

The dark green uniform worn by the 95th, and by the rifle companies and 6th Battalion of the 60th Foot. This was in imitation of the corps of sharp-shooters recruited from the huntsmen or jägers of the German forests, who wore on military service the same traditional and practical green clothing that they wore in their peacetime occupation. (Another German-imported custom was the moustache, worn at this time only by riflemen and Hussars, whose style of uniform was also copied from the Continent.) Officers of Rifles wore a uniform based on that of the Hussars, with a braided jacket, fur-trimmed pelisse, curved sword, barrelled waist sash, and tasselled Hessian boots. Rifle regiments, like Fusiliers, eventually saw the rest of the army equipped with their own special weapon; but, at this time, they alone were armed with the muzzle-loading Baker rifle. Tactically, they operated in the same way as the light infantry. The black collar, cuffs and shoulder-straps outlined in white braid were peculiar to the 95th, the 60th wearing red facings. Note the special black rifleman's equipment, with its distinctive silver 'snake' belt-buckle; the cord fastened to the cross-belt of the cartridge pouch supported a flask of fine-grain powder, used for loading and priming the rifle when there was leisure to do so. At other times the normal paper-wrapped cartridge is thought to have been used. Note also the brass-hilted Baker rifle sword-bayonet.

C2 Portuguese Rifleman, 5th Caçadores, campaign dress, 1811

The Portuguese army was completely re-organized and trained from 1808 by British officers and N.C.O.s, under the supreme command of William Beresford. They soon became extremely reliable troops, capable of operating as a matter of course in mixed divisions with British Line formations. The Caçadores were the light troops, equivalent to British Riflemen, French Chasseurs à Pied and German Jägers. Some were armed with the Baker rifle, others with muskets. The basic brown uniform had different coloured facings and decorations according to unit, and exact cut seems to have varied, according to surviving illustrations of the period. This figure is based on a reconstruction in the Lisbon Military Museum.

C3 Corporal, Portuguese 8th Infantry, full dress, 1810

Although the Portuguese conformed in general terms with British patterns of uniform and were, in fact, supplied with them largely from the looms and mills of northern England, they kept their own particular distinctions – notably the blue coatees of the infantry, and the distinctively shaped shoulder-straps. Grey trousers, in the British style, were often worn on active service, although the uniform illustrated officially included blue breeches and high black gaiters (see C2). The rank distinction of the Cabo or corporal is the double gold stripe around the cuff, and the sabre with yellow or gold sword-knot. The colours of collar, cuffs, and piping varied according to regiment; they were dark blue, yellow, and red respectively for this unit, the 8th (Castello de Vide) Line Infantry. Light companies wore the same uniform with a brass *cor-de-chasse* replacing the national arms on the shako, and a green fringe on the outer edge of the shoulder-straps.

D1 Corporal, Grenadier Company, 42nd of Foot (Royal Highland Regiment or Black Watch), service dress, 1810

The Highlanders wore many distinctions of uniform based on their national dress, but otherwise conformed to the rest of the army. Thus the corporal illustrated has two chevrons, and wears the white hackle and wings of the grenadier company. The 42nd had the privilege of wearing red plumes, so their grenadiers had white with red tips. The dark blue facings identify a 'Royal' regiment. The diamond-ended or 'bastion' loops were worn by several units, including the Royal Artillery and Royal Sappers and Miners. The feather bonnet could be fitted with a detachable peak, like that of a shako, for active service. Officers of Highland regiments carried a Scottish broadsword, and mounted officers wore tartan trews and a plaid. Officers and sergeants of Highland regiments wore their sashes over the left shoulder. (For further details, see the Men-At-Arms title *The Black Watch*.)

D2 Officer, 52nd Light Infantry, service dress, 1814
Light infantry regiments were dressed and equipped in much the same way as the light infantry companies of Line battalions. Thus they wore shoulder wings, and the green plume, and the officers carried curved swords and did not wear the gorget. The stovepipe shako continued in service with the light and rifle regiments when the rest of the infantry adopted the Belgic style, and remained the headgear of these élite corps until 1816. The sergeants carried light muskets instead of spontoons, and both sergeants and officers used whistles to signal orders in the field. These were carried attached to the crossbelt by a metal chain.

D3 Colour Sergeant, 11th Foot, full dress, August 1813
The rank of colour sergeant was introduced in July 1813. There was only one to each company, and the appointment, intended to improve the career structure of the non-commissioned ranks (always a pet reform of the Duke of Wellington) corresponded to that of the modern company sergeant-major. The badge of rank was worn on the upper right arm: a crown above a Union Flag, below which were two crossed swords, and below this again a single chevron. The three chevrons of a sergeant were worn on the left arm. N.C.O.s wore chevrons on both arms, with a gap of about half an inch between them; corporals wore two, sergeants three, and sergeant-majors (corresponding to the modern regimental sergeant-major) four. Sergeants wore scarlet coats like those of officers, instead of the madder-red of corporals and privates. Their distinctive weapon was the spontoon or short pike; in general usage this continued to be referred to as a halberd, although the true halberd – a pike with an axe-head – had been replaced by the spontoon in the 1790s. Additionally, sergeants were armed with a sword of the same type as that carried by their officers; and, like them, wore a crimson waist sash, although sergeants' sashes had a central stripe of the regimental facing colour.

E Private, 10th (Prince of Wales's Own Royal) Regiment of Light Dragoons (Hussars), campaign dress, 1814
Originally hussars were a branch of light cavalry raised from the half-wild mounted herdsmen of the Hungarian plains; and a number of distinctive items of dress, evolved in accordance with local fashion and working conditions, were later taken up by military tailors and adapted into more formal styles. The braided waistcoat became the laced hussar jacket; the wolf-skin worn around the shoulders as protection against the weather became the fur-trimmed pelisse; the fur cap with a long 'night-cap' bag became the fur busby with a flat bag hanging down one side; and the cords worn around the waist became a corded gold sash clasped together with crimson 'barrels' or hoops. The gradual adoption of these items by some regiments of British Light Dragoons was recognized in 1805, when the 7th, 10th and 15th regiments were permitted to add the suffix 'Hussar' to their title. The 18th were converted in 1807. Despite their flamboyant uniforms and continental moustaches, their tactical employment remained identical to that of conventional Light Dragoons. Note that this trooper is wearing his pelisse over his laced jacket for warmth. Leather trouser cuffs were not uncommon among both cavalry and dismounted troops in the field, and leather inserts on the inside of the leg were normal for the mounted branches.

F1 Officer, 9th Light Dragoons, parade dress, 1812
Most of the British Army's light cavalry work – reconnaissance and patrolling – was done by the Light Dragoons. The uniform illustrated was introduced in 1811 and was in fact less functional than that worn previously: the bell-topped shako so closely resembled that already in use by the French light cavalry that the possibility of mistakes under campaign conditions was considerable. The coatee had short tails reaching to the saddle, and the lapels were usually worn buttoned back to give the effect of a plastron or cloth breastplate. When worn in this way they were buttoned back all the way down to the waist, and the coatee was fastened in the centre with hooks and eyes. The cap lines were to prevent the shako being lost while galloping, and terminated in tassels and 'flounders' or knots of cord, plaited in the shape of the flat fish whose name they borrowed.

F2 Private, 3rd Dragoon Guards, service dress, 1814
Until 1811 British heavy cavalry (the Life Guards, the Royal Horse Guards, Dragoon Guards and Dragoons) wore the large cocked hat, long-tailed coatees with looped button-holes on the chest, cuffs and collar, white breeches and high boots. However, regiments on active service had generally worn various types of forage caps as headdress; and overalls, buttoned over boots and breeches, were common for some years before this point, when they were officially sanctioned for all mounted personnel on active service. For parades and reviews boots and white breeches remained the rule for all mounted officers and cavalrymen. The 1811 reforms included a new heavy cavalry coatee without loops, and fastened down the middle with hooks and eyes. Dragoons had pointed cuffs, Dragoon Guards square ones. Heavy gauntlets were worn. The metal helmet, resembling the Romanesque patterns used by French cavalry formations, had a bearskin crest curling forward for the Household Cavalry, and a flowing horsehair tail in the Line Cavalry. The brass chin-scales were not entirely decorative, as they gave a degree of protection from horizontal cuts to the throat and face.

F3 Gunner, Royal Horse Artillery, service dress, 1810
The Horse Artillery continued to wear this uniform – based on that of the Light Dragoons before 1811 – until after the Napoleonic Wars. The shell jacket was in the artillery colours of blue with red facing and gold lace, and the black helmet with the fur crest also bore the artilleryman's white plume. The numerous rows of loops were a Light Dragoon characteristic before the adoption of the coatee. Officers of the R.H.A. wore a hussar-type pelisse trimmed with brown fur, and all ranks wore the sabretache, or wallet, when this was introduced into the cavalry in 1811.

G1 Officer, Marching Battalion, Royal Artillery, service dress, 1814
The Royal Artillery at this time conformed to infantry patterns of dress in most respects; the major difference was that they traditionally wore blue coats, as servants of the Board of Ordnance, rather than red, as soldiers of the monarch. They wore the white plume of grenadiers.

G2 Gunner, Royal Artillery, service dress, 1810
The gunner wore the infantryman's stovepipe shako until 1812, when both arms adopted the Belgic pattern. The diamond-ended or 'bastion' loops were worn by all Ordnance Corps, as well as by a few infantry regiments. The pouch belt carried a small hammer and prickers, and the red cord carried a powder flask for priming. The sword bayonet was the most common personal weapon carried by the gunners of field batteries; one or two light muskets were carried on the limber for use in emergencies or by sentries. Gunners of garrison batteries carried muskets and infantry equipment, to defend their guns if the enemy came too close for the fixed armament to bear on them.

G3 Sapper, Royal Sappers and Miners, service dress, 1814
This sapper wears ordinary infantry pattern uniform, with the white plume and bastion loops of an Ordnance Corps. The red coatee with blue facings came into use in 1813; prior to this, the army's few sapper units had worn a blue coatee similar to the artillery pattern, with black facings. The change to red was ordered to make the sappers less conspicuous when serving with infantry working parties.

H1 Field Officer, Royal Engineers, service dress, 1811
The Royal Engineers were at this time an all-officer corps, selected from those cadets who came highest in the final order of merit at the Royal Military Academy, Woolwich. Engineer and artillery commissions could not be purchased, but depended on completing the R.M.A. course. They were therefore a type of specialist staff officer, and wore the cocked hat rather than the shako.

H2 Pioneer, Line Regiment, 29th Foot, service dress, 1811
The pioneers of the infantry provided local engineer support, obstacle clearance, and so forth. The grenadier cap could be worn with or without a peak, and with several minor variations of shape and size. The other distinctions of appearance were the felling axe, the leather apron, and the beard – in an otherwise clean-shaven army.

H3 Drum Major, 57th Foot, ceremonial dress, 1812
The drum-major illustrates the widespread – and international – convention by which trumpeters, drummers and bandsmen wore the colours of their regiment reversed; i.e., if the regiment had red coats faced with yellow, the musicians wore yellow coats faced with red. Drummers and bands of marching battalions wore shoulder wings (as they still do) and heavily laced coatees. The trumpeters of cavalry units wore especially ornate uniforms, carrying on the traditions of the heralds of chivalry. Musicians usually wore the normal headdress of the company or regiment to which they belonged with various embellishments, except for the drum-major, who was distinguished by a feathered cocked hat. He wears the infantry sergeant's sword and sash, and a baldric, richly laced, bearing two miniature drum-sticks. The brilliant uniforms of trumpeters and drummers not only looked impressive on parade but fulfilled a useful tactical purpose; it was important for an officer to be able to pick them out quickly to sound field calls in battle.